Keys to Understanding
Soul Ties, Soul Power,
& Soulish Prayers

Keys to Understanding
Soul Ties, Soul Power,
& Soulish Prayers

Liberty Savard

Bridge-Logos *Publishers*

Gainesville, Florida 32614 USA

SOUL POWER, SOUL TIES & SOULISH PRAYERS

by Liberty Savard

Copyright © 2001 by Liberty Savard
Library of Congress Catalog Card Number: Pending
International Standard Book Number: 0-88270-845-7

Bridge-Logos *Publishers*
PO Box 141630
Gainesville, FL 32614
http://www.bridgelogos.com

DEDICATION

This book is dedicated to all who seek to understand how to best cooperate with God's empowerment to bring their own souls into surrender to His divine will.

When we embrace His Word, His promise to us is:

> *"You welcomed it not as the word of mere men but as what it truly is, the Word of God, which is effectually at work in you who believe—(dash)— exercising its superhuman power in those who adhere to and trust in and rely upon it"*
>
> *(1 Thessalonians 2:13, Amplified).*

CONTENTS

INTRODUCTION

A human being's spirit and soul are two separate entities residing within the human body—man's three-part makeup. The human spirit longs for communion with its Creator, knowing that it belongs to God. The body is just a vessel. The unsurrendered human soul seems to believe the entire human being belongs to it! Misconception number one!

The human soul contains a hidden deposit of great natural power which, for the most part, is latent (dormant). God and Satan both want to use this power to fulfill their purposes for mankind.

- ***Satan—for purposes of spreading control, evil, and wickedness among mankind.***
- ***God—for purposes of expanding His Kingdom principles to bring abundant life, divine blessing, and Kingdom opportunities to mankind.***

The human soul ignorantly continues making its own self-centered plans, believing it is in control of its self-destiny. It sees no need to be concerned about any other purposes that might involve it. Misconception number two!

The unsurrendered human soul usually chooses to run from God, *"Because the carnal mind is enmity against God; for it is not subject to the law of God, nor indeed can be"* (Romans 8:7, *NKJV*). To run away from God is to run directly towards the enemy's plans. Running towards God is to run away from the enemy's plans. The unsurrendered soul is generally quite oblivious to this distinction. Misconception number three!

The human soul can be identified as the mind (the ability to think), the will (the ability to make decisions), and the emotions (the ability for feelings).

Thayer's Greek/English Lexicon speaks of the rational part of man as being "the power by which a human being feels, thinks, wills, and decides—the soul." Thayer also speaks of that part of man that "has the power of perceiving and grasping divine and eternal things, and upon which the Spirit of God exerts its influence"—the human spirit. Martin Luther said the human spirit is the "highest and noblest part of man, which qualifies him to lay hold of incomprehensible, invisible, eternal things."

This distinct separation of soul and spirit helps explain an experience most Christians will admit they have had—standing in a service going through the motions of praise and worship, yet feeling dry and empty. While our souls are still unsurrendered to God, they do not want to get up close and personal with Him in a worship experience. They will circumvent doing so in any way that they can. Our unsurrendered souls will throw up worry, fear, anxiety, and other negative emotions to prevent us from worshiping in truth and spirit.

All born-again believers have a surrendered, submitted, regenerated human spirit in communion with the Spirit of God. This is one issue that is settled, and we can cling to it with certainty, no matter what else seems to be happening in our lives! These same born-again believers often struggle with trying to force their human souls (minds, wills, emotions) to surrender the files of their traumatic memories, mind sets, wrong attitudes, and carnal understanding.

When Jesus spoke to the woman at the well in John 4:24, He told her that God desired to be worshiped in spirit and truth. In the *Amplified Version* of Isaiah 45:19, we can read that when God said He spoke in truth, He w as saying there w as a <u>straightforward correspondence between His words and His deeds</u>.

> ***There is little truth in worship unless the soul's words, deeds, and feelings are in agreement with the worship being offered to God. God desires the agreement of the spirit and the soul to truly magnify Him.***

There is hope, however, for the soul—<u>once it is surrendered to God</u>. *Thayer's Greek/English Lexicon* says (in #5590.2b) that the human soul "by the right use of the aids offered it by God, can attain its highest end and secure eternal blessedness." The unsurrendered soul can attain nothing of blessed eternal value on its own merits. Jeremiah 17:9-10 tells us that the Lord said, *"The heart is deceitful above all things, And desperately wicked; Who can know it? I, the LORD, search the heart, I test the mind, even to give every man according to his ways, According to the fruit of his doings"* (*NKJV*). The word used here for heart is the Hebrew word *leb,* which means the feelings, the will, and the intellect.

Your born-again spirit is God-conscious. Your unsurrendered soul is self-conscious and self-centered. Your body has a sensory (taste, smell, touch, sight, hearing) consciousness of its natural environment. Until your soul has been totally surrendered to the will and purposes of God for your life, it will dominate the choices you make about whether you will most closely relate with the supernatural spiritual realm of God or the earthly, comfort-driven realm of the world.

I believe Adam originally had astounding natural ability and power in his soul. It is not difficult to understand that this ability and power was like a magnet to the devil. Satan has always initiated his works of darkness through the souls of men and women first, then through their physical bodies. Sin is conceived in the mind, chosen by the will, and then manifested through physical responses and actions.

After the Fall in the Garden of Eden, God diminished Adam's <u>ability to use</u> the formerly accessible power of his soul. Watchman Nee wrote that God did not remove this power from the soul, but He made it <u>latent</u> (hidden, inactive, having a dormant potential). For the most part, man has not figured out how to tap into but a little of this latent power.

Through meditation practices designed to reach the hidden parts of man's soul, man (spurred on with Satan's help) has kept trying to find this power lurking within himself. Many cults and "religions" exist just to teach this form of introspective rummaging around in the unsurrendered soul's subconscious.

> *Men and women who have successfully accessed their own soul power have always caused destruction and loss of lives through its use.*

The practices of Eastern religion and many New Age groups are always focused on releasing this soul power. Jezebel, Hitler, Jim Jones, David Koresh, all used their understanding of soul power to seduce, intimidate, and control other human souls. Any soul power released through man's own efforts has never been used for God's purposes, regardless of how "spiritual" the means appear to be. The end result or desire is always for human control.

Christians are not immune to the lure of this untapped inner power!

Jim Jones (who led his followers to drink cyanide-laced Kool-Aid in a mass suicide in Guyana) came from a Christian ministry family. So have many other cult leaders who allowed the power potential of their own souls to become so important to them, they could not surrender it to God. Nearly everyone has tapped into some of this power of the soul at one time or another— by intimidating someone, playing mind games, manipulating others, deliberately making someone cry, even just the act of staring someone down. This is like a child playing with the toes of a sleeping evil giant.

After the Fall, which caused a severing of the human spirit to the Spirit-of-God because of mankind's sin, the "liberated" soul began to flex its mental muscles and ratchet up the power of its will. Still, as incredibly strong-willed as some human souls can be, they are like rocket engines just barely idling—for the time being. Enormous power to control and overrun others' lives lies lurking within the deepest areas of all souls not fully surrendered to God.

When you accepted Christ's sacrifice for your sins and became a believer, only your spirit became perfectly aligned to the Spirit of your Creator. Your soul stepped back, recognized trouble was brewing for it, and dug into its trenches for what it perceived to be the fight of its life.

> **The human soul *is not* renewed, saved, or set free of its wrong patterns of thinking, its deception and denial, and its self-agendas because of a spiritual salvation experience. The soul must choose to surrender itself to the will of God. You can cause your soul to do this.**

In Ephesians 2:10, *Amplified Version*, Paul tells the Ephesian believers, *"For we are God's (own) handiwork (His workmanship), recreated in Christ Jesus, (born anew) that we may do those good works which God predestined (planned before hand) for us, (taking paths which He prepared ahead of time) that we should walk in them—living the good life which He prearranged and made ready for us to live."*

Our souls have tried to follows their own paths, kind of like little trains chugging around without any tracks. Sometimes our soul trains ended up in the ditch, sometimes in the desert, and sometimes in the swamp. It is rough going when you have no clear set of tracks to run on.

> **God has laid down preordained tracks for us to follow, but they exist only in heaven—_until_ we reject our aimless wanderings in the desert and in the swamp, and cry out for His paths, His will, His ways. That brings us into alignment with the divinely laid tracks of our destiny.**

You begin to align with God's destiny tracks every time you bind your will to His will, crying out, "Not my will, but thy will be done in my life, Lord!:

Paul said to the Philippians <u>believers</u>: *"Wherefore, my beloved, as ye have always obeyed, not as in my presence only, but now much more in my absence, <u>work out your own salvation with fear and trembling"</u>* (Philippians 2:12, *KJV*). Paul was admonishing believers here, people whose spirits are already saved—people who had been born again. Yet, Paul told them there is a working out still required, and it is a serious thing—to be done with fear and trembling. It was the salvation of their souls.

Paul also told the Roman <u>believers</u> that all things were not completed and made new at the point of their spiritual salvation—there was more to be done in their souls: *"Be not conformed to this world: but be ye transformed by the renewing of your mind, that ye may prove what is that good, and acceptable, and perfect, will of God"* (Romans 12:2, *KJV*).

Jesus Christ, however, has presented all men and women with a divine Overseer for their lives; His shed blood creating a bridge to spiritual communion with the Father again. Jesus did not come to enslave the souls of mankind, rather He came to set them free from their own futile attempts to find power, possessions, and peace. He came to give mankind a better choice, the choice to live our lives with the power of His love.

God reveals himself spiritually through the born-again spirits of men and women, but our human souls came into this world being out of alignment with His plans. All babies are born with darkened understanding in unformed minds which are alienated from the mind and purposes of God. Read Ephesians 4:18 and Colossians 1:21, which refer to the state of the soul of non-believers.

Each baby's tiny soul, so often formed and molded by other darkened souls alienated

from God, has little chance of naturally drawing right conclusions about themselves, others, and God. This is why every individual born into this world needs to be spiritually born again to receive the light of Jesus Christ.

Only when the flawed human soul surrenders all of its own tracks and self-agendas to God does it become aligned with the destiny tracks God has for it. That soul is put "on-line" with God's plans. It becomes capable of receiving, translating, and imparting to others what God has poured into the born-again spirit. The human soul is meant to be the surrendered instrument that conveys God's love, mercy, wisdom, and understanding to those who are lost and dying.

Think for a moment about what touches other peoples' lives about your relationship with God. Is it watching you as you pray? Is it watching your spirit lost in communion with your heavenly Father? Is it seeing you read the Word? No. People become responsive to the presence and working of God when:

- *Watching your face radiating peace in the middle of a crisis.*
- *Watching your mouth speak calming words of grace and mercy in the middle of chaos.*

- ***Watching you choosing to respond with love and understanding in the midst of being verbally abused.***
- ***Watching you put your arms around a dirty street person and hold them tight while assuring them that God loves them.***

This is what the hurting, needy people see of your relationship with God—God working through your mind, will, and emotions to reveal His love, joy, and peace to them.

Nearly 2000 years ago, Matthew wrote that Jesus said He was giving the Keys of the Kingdom to His people (16:19, 18:18). Then Jesus said, *"Whatsoever you bind on earth will be bound in heaven, and whatsoever you loose on earth will be loosed in heaven."* These few words contain powerful prayer principles that can bind things on earth into alignment with God's already established will in heaven. Remember that Jesus said we should pray, *"Thy will be done on earth as it is in heaven"* (Matthew 6:10; Luke 11:2, *KJV*).

Many Hebrew and Greek words for "bind" and "binding" have positive meanings—tie, put oneself under obligation to, weave together, heal, undergird, hold, persuade, and cause fragmented pieces to coalesce and become one whole again. I believe this is a far more exciting and positive use of this powerful key than continually trying to bind up evil spirits.

The word "loose" in the original Greek, *luo,* (and companion words *rhegnumi* and *agnumi*) mean untie, break up, destroy, dissolve, melt, put off, wreck, crack to sunder by separation of the parts, shatter into minute fragments, disrupt, lacerate, convulse with spasms, break forth, burst, rend, tear up. These are strong words that a determined prayer warrior can accomplish great things with!

In J. B. Phillips' introduction to Dr. Alfred Marshall's *Greek/English Interlinear New Testament,* Phillips states he was quite pleased that Dr. Marshall had not missed the peculiar Greek construction of Matthew 16:19. Phillips said this verse was "not a celestial endorsement that God would bind and loose in heaven whatever we had bound and loosed on earth." Rather, the keys of binding and loosing were our means of coming into agreement with already established heavenly purposes.

> *These powerful Keys of the Kingdom are our means of coming into agreement with God as we pray that His already established will in heaven will be manifested on earth.*

xxi

The <u>Key of Binding</u> that Christ has given to His people is the:

1.   ***steadying,***
2.   ***stabilizing,***
3.   ***seat belt, and***
4.   ***safety harness key.***

As God's children, we can bind our wills to the will of God, our minds to the mind of Christ, and ourselves to the truth of His Word. One of the meanings of the word *bind* is to <u>put oneself under obligation</u> to someone (or some thing). I really like the idea of having a spiritual power key to use in prayer when I need to put my sometimes unruly will under obligation to God's will!

This key of binding will snug you up close and personal to God for perhaps the first clear look you have ever had regarding His will for your life. A one-time prayer does not keep you there, however. As long as your soul is still unsurrendered to God in any area, it will try to weasel itself out of any contact with His will. It will renew its attempts to distract you from pursuing God's plans and purposes for your life.

The <u>Key of Loosing</u> is the:

1. ***self-surgery on the soul,***
2. ***severing personal bondages,***
3. ***slashing wrong patterns of thinking, and***
4. ***spiritual warfare key.***

Loosing is a powerful prayer key for cutting the industrial-strength Velcro ties to the stuff your unsurrendered soul still clings to. Loosing prayers will clear out the old junk your mind loves to feed on and the grave clothes your soul insists upon draping itself with. Loosing prayers also wreak spiritual terrorism on evil spirits, and loosing prayers destroy stronghold doors the enemy accesses to harass you. Read more about spiritual terrorism in ***Keys to Understanding Spiritual Understanding & Warfare*** (Liberty Savard, Bridge-Logos Publishing, 2001).

This mini-book has been created to give understanding on how to pray with the Keys of the Kingdom to turn the heart (soul) of man to obedience and service to God. The questions and answers of so many who are struggling with the issues of the soul have been taken from my internet web site's Q&A ministry as well as from questions coming into our office by phone and mail. These people have helped me to understand the need for such a ministry dialogue.

1

SOUL TIES

Question: *Exactly what is a soul tie?*

Liberty's Answer: *Soul ties* are birthed when you enter into a wrong agreement with someone else. Wrong agreements range all the way from soulish prayers prayed together with others to wrong agreements to commit fornication and violent crime. I'm unsure where soul ties "operate," but I am very grateful that we can learn to recognize them and break them with the Keys of the Kingdom.

There are times when you are in a crisis and you need to just get out of it. If you are in a house on a cliff and an earthquake starts, the logical course of action is run for your life—away from the cliff. It is not logical or intelligent to go to the bookshelf or get on the internet to try to learn how earthquakes operate. You can do that later if you manage to get out of your cliff house alive. We don't always remember our priorities in a crisis.

I will never forget seeing a poster of a very harried looking person flailing around in a swamp, with the caption over his head: *It is hard to remember, when you're up to your neck in alligators, that your original purpose was to drain the swamp.* To me, this is saying a lot about remembering that you should deal with the source of the problem (the swamp), rather than just fighting continually with the symptoms (the alligators). Break the soul tie and the symptoms will begin to go away. Break the soul tie and let God worry about the details.

Question: *How can you tell if a soul tie has been formed?*

Liberty's Answer: Christians can enter into a soul tie without being fully aware of what they are doing, but there will always be some kind of warning from the Holy Spirit. That check might be just a vague sense of uneasiness that something is not right. I always perk up my spiritual ears when I feel an uneasiness. But I am also careful to loose any soulish reactions that might be masquerading as spiritual uneasiness. Do this by loosing all deception and distraction from your soul, after binding your mind to the mind of Christ.

Take note if you feel you need to contact another person whenever you feeling overwhelmed, or you are in an emotional state of fear or anger. Begin to question why you want to contact this person rather than going before the Lord to ask for direction and help. Soul ties always cause us to look horizontally towards the one we have the tie with, rather than to look vertically to our Creator. If you find that you are easily influenced by another person, or that you will change your ideas or beliefs because you feel this persons' ideas and beliefs are better, you may have a soul tie with them.

I believe the Holy Spirit specifically warns us when we do not grasp the serious consequences of an impending action we are choosing to make. When we choose not to heed His warning signs, it is because our souls, perhaps even the souls of others, have so much control in our lives. Your spirit always hears what God is saying, but a strong unsurrendered soul can block recognition of a warning that a wrong choice is about to be made.

There are times when God chooses to let you go through hard consequences that come out of making wrong agreements. Sometimes, when serious derailments of your destiny are inevitable if you go any further, God will send a powerful message. It may be a very difficult situation or hard circumstance that even your soul cannot block out or deny. If there is life-threatening danger involved, He may well set up circumstances to knock you out of the situation. I know that for a fact, as He once used a very large moving van to physically knock me out of a very dangerous circumstance I was in denial of.

There are many things Christians have believed to be acts of the devil that have been God's stopgaps in a downward slide of ultra-serious consequences. If He has to, God will use hard things on hard heads to save them from hard fates.

Question: *Aren't there good soul ties? Like between family members and parents and children?*

Liberty's Answer: There is *no* such thing as a good soul tie. Not with a prayer partner, not with a spiritual leader, not with a spouse, nor with our children. Whenever you are involved in a soul tie with someone, that other person is your first choice of agreement on issues. God comes in second, perhaps even third or fourth. Even a soul tie between husband and wife is wrong because it always puts God second, keeping Him out of the center of their relationship.

Christian parents can have soul ties to their children. These parents seem to function well in their own spiritual walks <u>until</u> something happens in the lives of their children. Then they seem to almost self-destruct in panic and fear. One Christian mother calls me periodically about a son who is in and out of jail, in and out of drug addiction, in and out of all kinds of things. Every time he gets into serious consequences, he pulls on the soul tie to his mother, and she runs and rescues him. The wrong agreement here is that she believes he really needs her to rescue him. But he's really using her to be able to remain the way he is, living as he chooses.

This mother once said to me, "When everything is all right in Frank's life, my faith is just fine. When Frank is in trouble, it tears my faith apart. Why doesn't God see that!" I was amazed at this convoluted logic. I reminded her that you don't really need faith if you are very comfortable with how things are going. But true faith, genuine trust and confidence in God, would not allow itself to be torn apart because a child is in trouble. When your child is in trouble, you need to push into and rest in the trust and confidence that you have in God. You need to know that He is fully aware of what is happening with the child. You also need to accept and surrender to the truth that God may want to teach your child something from the hard circumstance.

I asked her to consider that she had a soul tie with her son that was justifying and rationalizing why she was enabling his behavior. She has a very hard time believing that her response to his needs had been enabling him to stay in the lifestyle he had chosen. I managed to convince her to pray binding and loosing prayers to break those soul ties once. But soul-tie breaking is not always a one-time breaking, especially when the other person keeps trying to reestablish it.

> ***If you are involved in a soul tie and you break it, the other person will usually attempt to reattach it. If you still want it, you will respond and come back into wrong agreement with this person.***

It is a quite amazing thing how soon the other person might try to make contact with you when you pray and break any soul ties you have. The contact usually comes in the guise of great concern for the one who has just broken the soul tie.

With regard to the parent/child relationship while children are still in the home and hopefully learning about God, the parent should be binding his or her own will to God's will regarding every decision and direction given to a son or daughter. Parents should also be binding the wills and the minds of their children to God's will and Christ's mind. The motivation of decisions made and directions given by the parents will be judged by God.

parenting young children

Parents should always be seeking to know if their decision will turn the child towards learning the will of God or if the decision was made simply to control the child's behavior. Ask yourself about every choice you make, "am I trying to teach them to obey God, or do I really just want to get this child out of my hair for awhile!"

If more parents continually sought God regarding their own motivation in the child rearing decisions they make, they would try to make choices for the benefit of the child—

rather than their own convenience. If this was the filter that every choice was run through and then acted upon, we would see children growing up with less resentment and unresolved anger in their souls today.

Question: *Why can't we have a soul tie with our spouse, if we are both careful to remember to put God first? I just don't understand how you can say that a soul tie between a man and his wife can be bad. They are already one flesh.*

Liberty's Answer: Perfect love in a marriage before God must come from the born-again spirits of a man and a woman. Love from spiritual unity never grows bored or disappointed or cold when time passes and circumstances change. This love continues to see the gift in the other person when the gift wrapping begins to fray and wrinkle.

The soul and the body express marital love, too, but the spiritual union between the husband and wife is the only thing that can be counted on never to change. Feelings that come from the soul are subject to change,

unless the soul becomes perfectly aligned with the spirit.

A soul tie between a husband and wife comes from a mutual agreement that the other partner is responsible for the meeting of personal needs, whether reasonable or otherwise. There are certain needs in wounded souls that no human being can ever meet. A meeting of some needs will certainly be accomplished in a marriage, for each partner is a gift to the other partner. But ties between the souls of the two partners cause a man and a woman to look to each other before they look to God. When one partner's dependency upon the other partner is excessive, this intense neediness begins to drain the partner who is expected to meet the needs. The progression of emotions in this type of dependency generally run from frustration to exhaustion to resentment to hatred.

Everyone enters into marriage with some unmet needs, unhealed hurts, and unresolved issues. These can create a daunting set of expectations for another human being to try to meet. It is unreasonable when a marriage partner is expected to meet all of the needs of a partner. The soul's deepest needs and worst wounds can never be fixed by anyone but God. When a soul tie is in place, the married partners place God second on the list of being necessary. Marriages turn sour when partners cannot meet each others' needs and God is not allowed to.

The best insurance against the disappointments and manipulation that is inevitable in a soul tie is to let God permanently heal you of your past traumas.

Question: *I was in a prayer meeting not long ago and suddenly burst into tears because of something casually said to me. I was so embarrassed. One of the women suggested that I might be in wrong agreement with some word curses spoken by an authority in my life. We agreed in prayer as I bound myself to the mind of Christ and the will of God, and loosed the effects and influences of all wrong agreements I had been a part of. She also encouraged me to loose any resulting soul ties, which I did. The prayers helped and I felt better by the time the meeting was over.*

Later that day, I learned that a friend several hundred miles away felt a major attack of concern for me at precisely the time I was loosing any soul ties affecting me. I remember that it was just before the meeting was to end at 3:00 p.m. Could this mean that I had a soul-tie with my friend? We have been praying together for God to remove some really bad leadership from my church, was this a wrong agreement?

Liberty's Answer: I ask these two questions of people regarding soul ties being present in their lives:

> 1. *Have you and anyone else come into agreement over things that cannot easily be proven to be scriptural?*
> 2. *Have you prayed anything with another person that you would hesitate to pray openly in front of your entire church?*

Anytime you come into wrong agreement, especially in the form of prayer, doors open in your soul that lead to soul ties being formed. The enemy also uses these doors, and can even use your wrong prayers to harass the one(s) you have prayed about. When my ministry staff and I seem to be under unusual attacks from the enemy, we always loose the effects and influences of all wrong prayers that have been prayed about us.

God calls and places His leaders, and God alone should direct the removal of any of His leaders. You should never pray in hopes of a dismissal of leaders because you think they need to go. You have no idea what God is doing behind the scenes of everyone's lives. You should be praying that God's will would be done in every person in the congregation. You should be binding all of them to His will, and loosing wrong agreements off of them.

When you came into agreement in wrong prayers about this, you created a soul-tie between you and your friend that needed to be broken. God, in His mercy, set up a situation where you would pray such a prayer at that meeting. You should thank Him for this. That truly was a divine supernatural intervention in the natural realm of your life.

In general, do not ever pray any prayers based upon personal opinions, legalistic judgments, or emotional feelings—yours or anyone else's. Most prayers about how God should straighten out other members of the body of Christ are almost always soulish prayers.

Question: *My brothers recently moved in with me, my boys, and my mother. Both brothers are homeless, but have custody of their children. My mother and I have been supporting them through their difficult times. One brother refuses to work, and while the other one does work, he never seems to have any money. This puts me in a difficult position. I have used money that should have gone to pay my bills to buy food to feed everyone. Both of my brothers know that my mother and I try to live as good Christians. I believe they are using our Christian charity to take advantage of us.*

12

They know that I will not do anything that could upset my mother who is 72 years old and has a bad heart.

Liberty's Answer: This is indeed a difficult situation. Your brothers' children could be in a much worse situation if you had not taken them into your home. Have you been praying the binding and loosing principles for everyone involved? Yourself, your mother, your children, your brothers, and their children? You need the wisdom of God to know what to do right now. It is important that you bind your mind to the mind of Christ, and loose any wrong beliefs, preconceived ideas, or feelings of obligation or guilt that are not from God. Keep reading the Word. It is really quite amazing how God's Word can work on so many levels to apply to our situations.

You implied that any action on your part to force your brothers to take responsibility might cause your mother's health to be affected. I believe you should pray and loose soul ties from all four of you. Do you have any unresolved guilt regarding your mother? Do you have any unresolved issues regarding your brothers?

Unresolved guilt can cause us to keep trying to make things right that are not our place to make right. Our souls can manipulate us

13

> ***into doing "right" things for the wrong reasons.***

Loose any wrong motives you might have for doing what appears to be an active expression of love. Bind yourself to God's will and ask Him to clearly direct you to follow it.

Question: *My fiancé is very attached to his mother. After his father passed away two years ago, he began to take care of all of her affairs, going on vacations with her, seeing movies together, etc. He became a Christian a few months ago and then we met. We each believe that we are gifts from God to each other, but his mother does not. She speaks very badly about me to him. If he and I have problems, he tells her everything that we have said. She treats him like a child. He puts his mother before me in all situations, and I feel that she is the one meeting all his emotional and psychological needs. Can you give me any advice?*

Liberty's Answer: You need to be praying the binding and loosing prayers found in ***Shattering Your Strongholds*** for yourself (pages 131 and 139), and your fiancé and his mother (page 171). You must be very careful about judging this woman's intentions and whether she and her son have a wrong relationship. They may have soul ties between them, but I am only hearing your perspective of their relationship. God is the only one who knows exactly what is going on here. Neither you nor I do.

Pray and loose all layers over the unmet needs, unhealed hurts, and unresolved issues in your own life so you can hear clearly from God. I'm concerned that you are allowing your soul and your fiancé's soul to influence you so much. Let God be God in all ways and in all timing, or you may find yourself in a very difficult situation. If this man is the mate God has chosen for you, you can step back and trust God to work things out. Stop making judgments and begin to pray right prayers. You are in a position where you can cooperate with God's work in healing everyone in this situation.

Question: *I have been very impressed with the binding and loosing stuff you have written about. Can someone pray and break a soul tie between other people who are not believers, or can a soul tie only be broken between the two people who have it?*

Liberty's Answer: I do not believe we can actually sever soul ties between other people, believers or non-believers. That must be done by one of the people involved in the soul tie. I believe praying to loose soul ties in others pressures the people involved, causing a continued awareness of the problem. You can especially disturb the existence of soul ties in another person's life (based upon my prayer answers and others' testimonies) <u>when all of the binding and loosing principles are being prayed faithfully for them</u>. This must be done without interjecting personal opinions, judgments, criticism, or praying prayers that go amiss.

Whatever ground our prayers gain, that ground must be held by speaking right agreements about the individuals we are praying for. Declare aloud and agree with God, and declare aloud and agree with others who understand the power of right agreement in prayer, <u>that these people will know the truth</u>. Declare that God's will is going to be done in their lives here on earth. Declare that they will know God's love. If you have told someone that these people reject God, then go to that person and say you have repented for saying that. Then declare to them that God's love is going to wear down any fear and doubt in their souls to draw these people to himself.

Question: *Do I just loose and break any soul ties, and then I will be fine?*

Liberty's Answer: When you are praying to loose the effects and influences of wrong agreements and resulting soul ties, then you need to confess right agreements that directly oppose your previous wrong agreement. Perhaps you agreed or vowed that you would never allow anyone other than one certain person to get close to you. Pray and loose that wrong agreement—wrong because it is not what the Word says we are to do. Then confess that you are going to let God teach you to trust others. Confess that you are going to offer to help others and not worry about whether or not they try to use you.

Begin to declare that with God you can love, you can trust, and you can reach out to others. Then take actions to confirm what you have said. Begin to speak in love and understanding when with difficult people. Begin to speak more kindly to others. Do something nice for others. Offer to help someone just because God would appreciate your having done so. Get the idea? God bless.

Question: *The person I've been dating (and was going to marry) broke up with me. I believe he has many deep hurts and I want to help. I love this person unconditionally and would do anything or make any sacrifice to see him healed. Will you pray for us to find our way back to each others?*

17

Liberty's Answer: Too often hurting and needy people think, "If I am willing to go through a lot of sacrifice and pain, then God will let me have a relationship with this person." These are the unhealthy words of an unsurrendered soul full of unmet needs. This soul believes that God would accept personal sacrifice and pain from one human in exchange for a gratitude-filled relationship with another human.

> *God did not create you to be a human sacrifice because He had no other way to heal and restore this other person. The Ultimate Sacrifice for every person's healing and wholeness has already been made!*

If we had the option of becoming sacrifices for other peoples' healings, would that not give our souls' control over the other people's lives? Would you want your healing and wholeness to be dependent upon someone else's willingness to sacrifice themselves for your destiny purposes? Probably not.

> *Begin to bind your will to the will of God and bind your mind to the mind of Christ. Bind yourself to the truth in the Word. This*

requires that you immerse yourself in the Word daily in order to hear the truth from God, not just to "use" the Word to find promises to try to hold God to! Loose the effects and influences out of your soul of every wrong agreement you have ever spoken, entered into, or believed. Loose your soul's efforts and agendas to get what it believes will fulfill you. Ask the Lord to work in you so that you will be healed, restored, renewed, and ready for His best!

We will pray for you that:

- **God's will which has already been set in place in heaven regarding each of you will be done on earth in each of your lives.**
- **Each of you will focus on tearing down strongholds so you can receive God's healing in your souls to be ready for what God does next.**
- **All soul ties between you and this man are loosed and broken.**
- **You will both be able to hear God's healing and guiding words clearly. This**

19

is very hard to do when you allow yourself to be consumed with your desperation, pain, unmet needs, and unhealed hurts.

• **God will give you great grace and mercy and understanding that He may have allowed or even caused this separation at this time. This gives God room to speak to and heal both of you.**

God is this man's Healer, Teacher, and Savior— not you, and God is not at a loss as to what to do here! You cannot make someone else surrender, but you can choose to surrender yourself.

God did not send His Son to die for you so that your future could be held hostage while you grieve over a stalled human relationship. God is always working His greater plans for your life.

Be willing to withdraw yourself from the line of this other person's destiny preparation. Trust that God will put your paths together or separate them according to His larger scope of purpose for both of you. Realize that you, in your finite way of viewing things, are looking through powerful filters of your own unmet needs and unhealed pain. These may create hindrances and delays that will cause unnecessary pain to yourself *if you try to stay soulishly involved in this phase of God's infinite work in another person's life.*

Peace and contentment are possible in all things, even while you may be feeling the emotional pain from the break in relationship. Fear and lack of trust in God often catapults people into wrong relationships. There is a prayer in ***Breaking The Power*** called the **"Training-Wheel Prayer to Prepare for a Mate."** Here are a few lines from that prayer:

> *I bind myself to your will, Father, and I ask you to show me how to purify my motives for a relationship. I do not want only want a relationship just to meet my unmet needs. Help me to understand that no man or woman could ever fulfill such unrealistic expectations. I do not want to force my way past your will into a relationship only to see my needs suck all of the joy, peace, and life out of a mate.*

> *I've felt trapped in a vacuum where nothing is ever enough. I don't want to be there*

anymore! No one will ever place their hope in a Christian whose life always seems unsatisfied, needy, and in pain. But many can receive hope from a life that was once like that—but has now been changed and made whole by you! I want to be changed and made into a source of hope and blessing to others.

Please forgive me for the times I have blamed you for my loneliness and for my not having some person who cares just for me. Jesus, if there is a special man/woman you have chosen and are preparing just for me, I bind him/her to your will and purposes. I ask that you draw him/her into a strong, whole relationship with you. I ask that you teach him/her to see you as the focus and center of his/her life, just as I am asking you to do with me. I bind myself and him/her to your timing. I will not seek to find any such person through my own efforts. You will know if and when the time is right for both of us to come together into a relationship. Amen.

Question: *Why would anyone want to have a soul tie with someone else?*

Liberty's Question: Soul-ties are the product of a wrong agreement that appears to hold a promise of <u>benefit</u> for each person involved. Even if one person feels forced or threatened into the wrong agreement, the "benefit" can be that something worse may have been avoided (i.e. humiliation from being exposed, loss of position because of taking a stand, blackmail, etc.).

Several years ago, I succumbed to old wrong beliefs that I would be misunderstood and accused of being rebellious if I resisted agreeing with a ministry leader who was using soul power to pressure me. I felt I had no choice at the time, which was not true, of course. The <u>benefit</u> I thought I saw in this wrong agreement was <u>acceptance, approval, and increased exposure on a ministry level</u>. I had "shot myself in the foot" so many times in my earlier days as an aggressive, opinionated new Christian that I had been accused of having a Jezebel spirit. I was deeply hurt and wounded by this, and I never knew how to let go of the unresolved issues of the accusation. So I accepted a guilt that was not mine to accept.

When nearly identical circumstance resurfaced in my life several years later, I made the wrong choice again. The moment the situation seemed to resurface, I remember fearing being accused of having a "Jezebel spirit" if I did not cooperate. The term, *Jezebel spirit,* is often used to control people. No such term exists anywhere in the Bible.

Satan is a master at <u>recreating copycat</u> <u>circumstances to mirror the past circumstances of your</u> <u>unresolved issues</u>. When difficult issues are not resolved correctly the first time, I believe he records all of the details surrounding them. Then he maneuvers peoples around until he gets just the right mixture and he reruns the copycat circumstance on you. There is a strong probability that the copycat issues will not be resolved correctly the second time, either—unless you have experienced healing and renewal within your soul by letting God into the unresolved issues it has tried to hide.

Question: *Can we have a soul tie with a dead person?*

Liberty's Answer: It is within the soul that grief is experienced. There is no such thing as a spirit of grief (see chapter 3 of **Breaking the Power**). If someone had a soul tie with a person who has since died, how strong that soul tie was and how unwilling the remaining person is to let go of it will determine how long the grieving will continue. God will extend all grace to empower us to acknowledge our loss, grieve for a period of time, and then surrender our grief to Him and get on with our lives. This does not mean we should never think of the person again, with love and perhaps bittersweet memories, for this is a natural thing to do.

However, the prior existence of soul ties will allow excessive grief to continue on and on. While these residual ties can be severed, those in extended grief often do not want to do so. These ties are the last remaining link they believe they have to the one now gone. These individuals often begin to see themselves as defined by their grief. The soul ties need to be loosed, breaking off the remaining soul's attempts to cling to something familiar about the person who has died. Soul ties are familiar. Once the soul ties are broken, then God's Spirit can pour healing and peace into the soul of the bereaved one.

Question: *I have a good friend and I love to pray with her. We think exactly alike on everything we are praying about. Is this okay?*

Liberty's Answer: It is okay as long as you are aware that people who think just like us are not always very good about speaking straight up truth to us. Sometimes the reason we like them and they like us is because everyone knows where each others' painful hot spots are and studiously avoids pushing them. We feel safe with these people. I think we should pray and ask God for prayer partners who will jerk us up short every time we think about praying amiss. A real friend does not let us avoid reality and truth, but instead will always speak to us in love when we are doing our best to go into denial.

The following prayer is a Training Wheel Prayer for Breaking Soul Ties.

> *Lord, I have made wrong agreements with other people. I have agreed to things I knew I should not, in hopes that I would get some sort of benefit that would ease my pain. I have allowed relationships with other people to get out of alignment with your will for me. I want to be free from all emotional, intellectual, and self-willed soul ties I have formed with others. Forgive me for allowing this to happen. Forgive me for having sought satisfaction and fulfillment from anyone except you.*

I now choose to bring my needs to you. I will no longer let fear overcome me when I feel alone and vulnerable. Instead, I will remember that this means I am in a place where my soul's walls and defense systems are down, and I will move towards you. Feeling vulnerable is a reaction to my soul feeling that it is out of control. This is a good place to be!

My spirit does not feel vulnerable, for it is connected to the Spirit of my Creator. Help me to always remember that. Come deep into my soul and touch every dark spot with your grace and mercy. My sense of vulnerability is an open door to your grace, God, no matter how quickly my soul might try to reestablish its protective barricades against you. If I am not sure of what I loosed that finally tumbled my soul's defenses, I'm not sure how long they might stay down.

A time will come when my soul's defenses will be completely gone, when it will surrender totally to you. But for now I will continue to loose its defense systems until they can no longer be reactivated. Increase my awareness of my unsurrendered soul trying to get its expectations met, and help me to act immediately. Increase my awareness of old patterns of behavior that I need to reject and to loose, so that I will not turn back to them when I feel frightened or needy.

No fear! No more fear! I bind myself to this truth. I will remember that fear is not a spirit—fear is the absence of trust and confidence in your goodness and love and power towards me. My spirit cannot fear, it is my soul that fears. Fear is an emotional reaction to the traumatic issues I have never allowed you to reach into and resolve.

Help me to know the truth that I do not need to feel any doubt or fear when you get close to the ugly things hidden in my soul. Help me to know that you already know what is in there, and you are not ashamed to walk into them with me. You will heal me from them once and for all. I've lived with ugly old "stuff" long enough! So, here I am! I'm ready! Amen.

2

SOUL POWER

I remember one minister asking me what I thought about a meeting we had just been in with a high-energy "power-preacher." I cautiously replied, "I think he was very impressive, but perhaps operating a little too much in soul power."

The other minister looked at me with surprise and said, "Liberty, if we didn't operate in soul power some of the time, we'd never get anything done for God." I shivered at those words, for I knew this made perfect sense to this minister and to others as well. Regardless of how seemingly great the end result might appear to finite thinking, no end will ever justify soulish means.

The unsurrendered soul's agendas are never for God's ultimate glory, they are always geared to receiving personal glory while throwing a few bouquets God's way. This is a fine line to walk, especially for the one who forgets that *"God is closely watching you, and he weighs carefully everything you do"* (Proverbs 5:21, *TLB*).

Question: *At a Christian conference not long ago, I was told some things seemed good. However, after going home and praying, I began to wonder. How do we keep from being deceived? I contributed a large amount of money to the ministry in question, I think mainly because of my emotions. I want to do what is right in case that ever happens again.*

Liberty's Answer: I, too, have been deceived in Christian "settings" in the past, all because something being presented from the pulpit appealed to my soul. It is getting hard to recognize some of the shades of off-white and pale gray in the soulish realm today— particularly in the world, but also in the Church. There is no "take this pill and you'll be fine" remedy to discerning the difference between truth and near truth.

Knowing how to discern truth only comes by consistently <u>doing, using, and acting upon</u> what you have read in the Word, heard preached, and received from the Holy Spirit in response to your seeking.

Bind your mind to the mind of Christ daily. Guard yourself against even partially wrong teaching by renewing your mind (Romans 12:1-2) with the washing of the Word of God daily. Everything that comes into your mind, pour it through the filter of the Word that you should be constantly feeding upon.

Proverbs 4:20-23 (*NKJV*) tells us that the Lord says to us, *"Give attention to my words; incline your ear to my sayings. Do not let them depart from your eyes; keep them in the midst of your heart; for they are life to those who find them, and health to all their flesh. Keep your heart (soul) with all diligence, for out of it spring the issues of life."* Remember to guard your soul (the heart), which you can do by binding your will to the will of God, binding your mind to the mind of Christ, and by binding your emotions to the comfort of the Comforter. Then loose wrong agendas, self-motives, wrong beliefs, and wrong patterns of thinking from your soul.

Further regarding this command to guard our souls because of them spring the issues of life, the commentator Matthew Henry says: "A good reason is given for this care (of the soul), because out of it are the issues of life. Out of a heart (soul) well kept will flow living issues, good products, to the glory of God and the edification of others. Our lives will be regular or irregular, comfortable or uncomfortable, according as our hearts (souls) are kept or neglected."

Tell the Lord in prayer that you want to learn how to know the truth, however He wants to teach it to you. Ask Him to help you practice discerning His truth in any issue. Trust Him to do so, especially if you are consistently filling yourself with the truth of His Word. How can He help you practice His Word if you are not filled with it?

Question: *I have been prophesied over many times. The last time was different, though, and I don't know what to make of it. I was told to leave my job and move to another state because God had a work there for me to do. This caught me completely by surprise. In the past when I've been given a word from the Lord, it has confirmed what I already knew. I trust the person who gave it, but how do I know for sure that it was from God and not from this person's soul?*

Liberty: People should wonder more than they do these days about every prophetic word they receive. Being concerned about a prophetic word being authentic does not have to cast negative judgment on the person who spoke it to you. Everyone makes mistakes, even prophets. Godly prophets will always tell you to pray about any words they give to you. We must submit everything prophesied to God and let Him sort it out.

No one has to come into agreement with a word given by anyone. This was something I had to be taught as a new Christian after suffering much anguish and fear over false prophetic words given to me. But one dear father in the faith said to me, *"[Liberty, just because someone says it does not mean you have to believe and receive it.]"* Paul said, *"Do not quench the Spirit; do not despise prophetic utterances. <u>But examine everything carefully</u>; hold fast to that which is good"* (1 Thessalonians 5:19-21, *NAS*). In this verse, the word *examine* means to prove something is true. All prophetic words should be prayed about, studied in the Word, and then taken before God for confirmation.

Use the binding and loosing Keys of the Kingdom to be sure you are in a right attitude within your own soul when you hear a prophetic word. There are times when the soul has an offense against another person, or a word spoken goes against a cherished soulish belief.

If that happens, a true word from the Lord could be rejected. If you are given a word "from the Lord" by someone you like very much, someone you want to like you, or someone you want to impress with your submission, you can accept a false word.

It is always a good thing to bind your will to the will of God and your mind to the mind of Christ, loosing soulish distraction and prejudice from yourself. And it is a good thing to renew that prayer whenever you are given a prophetic word. Your soul must be as under submission to the Spirit and as clear of prejudice as it can be to hear what God may really be speaking.

Some words spoken may not be true prophecy from the Holy Spirit, they may just be well-meant soulish exhortations couched in "God-language." The discerning of spirits is one of the gifts of the Spirit given to the believer. This gift is for spiritually knowing if a human soul, a demonic spirit, or the Holy Spirit is the source of a prophecy or a manifestation.

> *Watchman Nee says, "The greatest advantage in knowing the difference between spirit and soul is in perceiving the latent power of the soul and in understanding <u>its falsification of the power of the Holy Spirit</u>."*

We need to run spiritual reality checks on ourselves before we would prophesy as an oracle speaking for Almighty God. Most false prophecies are a result of preconceived soulish ideas looking for a public platform of expression. However, some false prophecies are prompted by evil spirits who have discerned open doors to harass someone through—both the one prophesying and the one being prophesied to.

Even the person who is just giving soulish, feel-good exhortations of comfort and promise has a wrong agenda (regardless of how loving they may seem). Their agenda may well be a desire for approval and acceptance, or just to cause someone to feel better. The prophet who prophesies that which is not popular can be very unpopular. Just ask Jeremiah when you get to heaven. The Jews threw him into a pit for prophesying that which did not make them feel good.

A prophetic word should usually be a revelation to the prophet as well, rather than a validation of what the prophet has been hoping God would say. Never judge a corrective prophecy give to someone or to a church by the fact that you have always felt someone needed to correct the person of church in just exactly that way. This would be is a soulish judgment on your part about 99.99 percent of the time.

Question: *I just read the Temptation article under the Difficult Issues page on your web site after I asked you to pray for my son who is addicted to pornography. Can we really pray these binding and loosing prayers for others—can I pray them for my son and loose this stronghold in him?*

pray for others

Liberty's Answer: The original meaning of loosing (of the Keys of the Kingdom, Matthew 16:19) is shattering, destroying, melting, tearing apart, etc. You cannot dismantle your son's strongholds or the soul ties he may have with others. However, you can thoroughly rattle and shake some of his wrong thinking that is supporting them. This almost always leads to some rethinking on the part of the one you are praying for.

The original Greek meaning of the word *stronghold* as it is used in 2 Corinthians 10:3-5 is the (human) logic and reasoning and arguments we use to defend our arguments (or our right to believe something). As you pray to shake up your son's strongholds, you can cause him to question whether or not he still wants them. As you pray and bind his mind to the mind of Christ and loose the grave clothes from him (read chapter on binding, and the chapter on loosing, in **Shattering Your Strongholds** for further information), you will free him to hear from Jesus Christ, if only briefly.

36

Question: *Why can't I stop fantasizing about things, and settle for what I have? What stronghold is involved here?*

Liberty's Answer: You have learned to comfort yourself with certain fantasy thought patterns, an internal form of mental and emotional stimulation. At some point during a traumatic or frightening time when you felt extremely insecure and lacking nurturing, you learned how to stimulate a sense of well being in yourself (mentally, emotionally, even physically). This self-stimulation can release endorphins within your body (the natural, internal "feel good" hormones our bodies and souls love). These endorphins are greedily received by the opiate receptors in your brain, just as drugs, alcohol, and the chemical breakdown of food are.

You probably have stronghold patterns of thinking that you have built to justify your beliefs that you are the only one who really cares about how you feel. These strongholds are also reinforcing and justifying your feelings that you have to do something to initiate your own sense of well-being. You may have even decided that God does not care whether or not you have any sense of well being.

Continue to bind your will to the will of God, bind your mind to the mind of Christ, and loose wrong thought patterns and beliefs you have, particularly about God. Loose all deception and denial that your soul is using to confuse you about His concern for you. Also loose the wrong mind-body agreement that you have that you need to act out certain behaviors (fantasy or otherwise) that will release endorphins to your brain. Loose and tear up the endorphin "tracks" that the repetition of these stimulated releases have etched into your brain. Renew your brain/mind, by the washing of the Word, that it would accept new spiritual means of satisfaction and good feelings in yourself.

> ***Therefore do not worry, saying, 'What shall we eat? or 'What shall we drink?' or 'What shall we wear?' For after all these things the Gentiles seek. For your heavenly Father knows that you need all these things. But seek first the kingdom of God and His righteousness, and all these things shall be added to you. Therefore do not worry about tomorrow, for tomorrow will worry about its own things. Sufficient for the day is its own trouble***
> (Matthew 6:31-34, *NKJV*).

Question: *Shattering Your Strongholds* is by far
the most useful book I have read in a long time. I felt
so much freedom after reading it. I recently heard
someone teach that a wife could not go any higher in
God than her husband goes, and that the wife's intimacy
with the Lord could only match the intimacy level of
her marriage. This teacher said that a woman was full
of pride if she thought otherwise. If one partner seeks
God and the other doesn't, do you believe God would
turn away the one who does? This has really upset me,
it is almost like she put a curse on me.

husband not a believer

Liberty's Answer: No, I do not believe what has
been said here is correct. That is an Old Testament form
of legalistic thinking. 1 Corinthians 7:13 (*NIV*) it says
that *"if a woman has a husband who is not a believer
and he is willing to live with her, she must not divorce
him. For the unbelieving husband has been sanctified
through his wife . . . ."* How could a believing wife
sanctify her unbelieving husband through her faith if
she could rise no higher than he was in God?

*There is no human authority—NONE—
established by God to stand between you and
Him. The belief that someone can or does has
been the foundation of many cults. Nothing*

39

can place a vertical interference into your relationship with God except you.

God has instituted authority in human relationships on earth, but it is a horizontal line of authority. It is never a vertical line with one human being able to place a cap on someone else's relationship with God. This horizontal line of authority runs between us and other humans, and it should always be exercised in love— never in control. We are all to respect and honor all others, whether they are in a position of authority or not.

> **"Let love be genuine; hate what is evil, hold fast to what is good; love one another with brotherly affection; outdo one another in showing honor"**
> (Romans 9-10, *RSV*).

This teacher's statement about pride sounds like an attempt to control. Still, you need to forgive her for what she has said, and pray for God to give her wisdom and understanding of the truth. Bind her mind to the mind of Christ and pray that God will reveal an understanding of grace and mercy to her. As she is a leader, she needs these attributes in abundance to lovingly minister to His lambs.

Always remember that God would never deny His presence to a true seeker because of another person's attitude towards Him. How would Christ have ever ministered to the woman by the well, with her five husbands, if He had not wanted to relate personally to her need for God? I think you should loose from your soul all of the effects and influences of any of this teacher's words about this issue, before it tries to grab onto them and build a memorial to them. I will help you pray for everyone who may still be confused about this.

Question: *My husband is a loud and argumentative man. He always yells at me when I don't want to do something. He yells and intimidates me until I agree to do it. I never have a choice.*

Liberty: Whenever a husband (or a wife) places himself (or herself) in a position of power between the other partner and Christ, the one doing so is operating out of the soul. Any time that the emotions are revving up, the will is digging trenches, and the mind is spewing out sarcasm and accusations, the soul's power is on parade.

Your husband is yelling to control you because it works for him. Your statement "I never have a choice" is not true. We often look at many of our tough choices through a veil of anxiety and apprehension: How will I be affected if I don't make the right choice? God looks at our tough choices as either

- ***a miracle-producing-process of acting by faith*** or
- ***a trip around the same mountain again because of not acting by faith***.

You have entered into a wrong agreement here that you are helpless to cause change in your marriage. You need to loose the effects and influences of that wrong agreement.

The soul initiating the wrong agreement is usually somewhat "*stronger*" than the other soul. The use of the word stronger is not intended to be descriptive of physical force, but of the source of the power drive in the soul. The stronger soul's drive may come from a reservoir of unmet needs and unhealed hurts. Either way, the stronger soul will position itself to manipulate other souls in order to get the response it believes it needs.

Bind your will and your spouse's will to the will of God, and bind both of your minds to the mind of Christ. Bind both of your souls to the awareness of the blood of Jesus Christ and its miracle working power. Loose wrong beliefs and wrong attitudes you may have towards your mate, and loose wrong beliefs and wrong attitudes he may towards you. Loose stronghold thinking from both of your souls.

Loose word curses (hard, cruel, negative words) that your mate may be speaking to you. Loose soul ties between you. Loose any fear you have. Ask the Lord to heal both your soul's and his soul's unhealed hurts and unmet needs. Ask the Lord to pour out grace and mercy upon both of you. There are times when an angry soul says, "I don't like/love you anymore." Or, "I can't stand you anymore." These words come from the unsurrendered <u>soul's bitterness and resentment that its expectations and needs have not been fulfilled and met</u>. No human being could ever meet these kinds of expectations. These prayer principles will help you help your husband to open up to receiving God's meeting of his needs.

You do have a choice to cooperate with God to bring healing into your relationship. Pray the excerpts from the Breaking Soul Power Prayer below to bring your own soul into alignment with God's will. The Keys of the Kingdom are near your hand—use them to begin to change yourself. Your husband will not be able to ignore the power of God in your changed life.

> *Bless the Lord, O my soul, with all that is within you. Bless His holy name! Soul, I bind you to your destiny as a fully surrendered and divinely created part of God's Kingdom purposes. I bind myself to the destiny that Christ has made possible for me through divine covenant relationship, a new spiritual family heritage, and a new bloodline. You, soul, will come into alignment with my divine destiny purposes.*

> *Soul, I loose (smash, destroy, rip apart) the wrong beliefs, wrong attitudes, and wrong patterns of thinking you have created to try to control my life. I loose all denial, deception, and discouragement from you. I loose the influences and effects of the word curses you have perceived as "truth." I loose the influences and effects of the wrong agreements and soul ties you have entered into.*

You, soul, were created by God to translate His revelation and understanding to the hurting of this world—you were not created to run my life! You will learn to delight in what God has in store for you. Through a renewed mind, healed emotions, and the courage of a surrendered will, you are going to bring forth answers and new understanding to many. You will cooperate with my regenerated spirit.

Mind, once you turned in circles like a rat caught in a maze, constantly going over and over decisions you had no answers for, yet you felt trapped into making. The unresolved issues you kept trying to bury crawled up out of their soulish graves again and again. Mind, I bind you to the realization of divine interventions occurring all the time in the problems you could never solve before—but now God solves while you sleep.

Emotions, forget not how you once reeled between laughter and tears, boldness and fear, hope and despair, affection and anger. You frightened people with tears of neediness

45

and outbursts of anger. You fueled my feelings of rejection, betrayal, and loneliness. You will now receive divine peace, embrace joy and hope, and respond to the Holy Spirit's lifting power when old, negative feelings try to ascend.

Will, forget not the causes and the battles you used to engage in, rigidly implacable and unrelenting in your stands. Unrepentant, unbending, unyielding, unwilling to work with others' ideas, you alienated many from me. You caused much grief with your stubbornness and rebellion to God's ways. But you are learning how to be strong, yet flexible; to be right, yet entreatable; to be bold, yet gentle; to be courageous, yet concerned for others. Only the Holy Spirit can perfectly balance these strengths in me.

Soul, you will surrender the barricades you have erected over the deepest, darkest chambers within me. I loose the self-denial, the self-protectiveness, the self-defense, and the self-centeredness protecting my vulnerabilities that are so needful of God's grace. I loose the lies and all guilt you have tormented me with over things that were not my fault. I loose the deceptions you have hammered me with and have used to cause me to cave in to your control.

Lord, may your truth always be the plumb line to true up my thoughts, feelings, and choices. I want your truth to be the straight edge of my spirit, the guiding light of my life, and the backbone of my soul. Bless the Lord, O my soul, with all that is within you. Forget not His benefits. Remember what He has done for you! Amen

3

SOULISH PRAYERS

A soulish prayer sounds good, feels good, and seems to state exactly what God should want to answer. Praying soulish prayers alone can lead you into all kinds of deception. Praying soulish prayers with others can land you in a soul tie with them. I believe you can also come into wrong agreement with an appealing lie from an evil spirit, forming a soul tie with it. Evil spirits don't have bodies of their own, but they do have the ingredients of a soul—minds, wills, and emotions. Read in Ezekiel 28 about Lucifer's intelligence, determination, and pride.

Many needy and unhappy Christians have cried out to God to bring them mates, money, recognition, fame, appreciation, even big ministries. The desperate hope that God will do this begins to falter when God does not, reinforcing a wrong belief that God doesn't love them enough to care. God cares very much, but He knows that what they are asking for will not fill their emptiness. He will not give what they *think* they need when it would only be a temporary panacea—ultimately creating more desperation.

If you believe that you must meet your own neediness, you will view others according to their value to for filling up your soul's emptiness. You will seek others who will agree with you for what you need, thereby setting up the potential for soul ties between unsurrendered souls. These wrong agreements are sought in many different areas, as revealed in the question below.

Question: *My church is dying, and I feel that I am at my limit. I have been patient with my pastor, telling him about your books and others on the end times. He is just not interested in them. I have also given your books to others in the church and these people confirm what I am saying. I will not cause disunity in my church, however I cannot deny that God* *has called me to encourage your material. I am prepared to hand in my resignation as a church leader over this issue, as I believe I have much to offer. I am ready to shake the dust off my shoes. What do you think?*

Liberty's Answer: It is time to go into the spiritual realm and pray the Keys of the Kingdom principles of prayer you have learned from and believe so strongly. Bind your mind to the mind of Christ, and loose the effects and influences of all wrong words that you have spoken about your pastor. You have been involved in wrong agreements about him, for you are saying that others in the church agree with you. You need to repent of having made them, and then begin to prophesy or speak right agreements over your church and your pastor.

Start by declaring that God's established will in heaven for the pastor and for this body of believers shall be done on earth. Declare that God's will shall be done in your life on earth, and that you are surrendering to whatever He wants you to do to repair any breeches that have come between the pastor and other believers.

Why are you so ready to resign? What if Christ had resigned from His ministry when He was rejected and betrayed? Perhaps you have been called to pray behind the scenes for your pastor without any recognition at all.

> ***Think about Joseph languishing in a prison for something he didn't do—Daniel in slavery in Babylon—Paul in the Roman prison. Each one of these men was in difficult to understand situations because God was positioning them for roles of influence and power in the future. What if they had bailed on Him during this process because they did not understand, and they felt they should shake the dust off their shoes?***

God is not appreciative of people trying to help Him reposition His spiritual leaders. 1 Corinthians 10:32-33, Paul said we should not let ourselves become hindrances to the church of God, leading others into sin by our actions and behaviors. I would urge you to hold steady and bathe your pastor in prayer, binding him to the will of God, while asking God to pour out grace and mercy upon him. Whatever you do, do not speak any further wrong agreements about him to anyone. God will respond to that in ways that can really complicate your life. We will be praying with you. Here is a sample prayer of how you can pray for your pastor:

Lord, I thank you for every single leader you have placed in our church. I ask you to give them inspiration, I ask that you stir up their anointing, and I ask that you bless them and cover them with grace and mercy. I bind them to your purposes, that they will walk in the center your will for our church and heavenly things will be accomplished on earth. I bind their minds to the mind of Christ, and I ask that you give them new understanding of your truth, that you pour out your wisdom upon them. I choose to believe that they will embrace your will and your truth and walk in their earthly destinies with great strength and power. I loose the assignments of the enemy from them.

I bind every person in our church, including myself, to your will for our lives. Teach us how to be more humble and aware of our own wicked ways, always seeking your face and speaking forth right agreement concerning your will for every person we know. Teach us how to break the power of all wrong agreements that have ever been spoken about this church and its leaders, teach us how to

always pray in agreement with your Word and your will for our leaders.

Your Word says to "Obey your leaders and submit to their authority. They keep watch over you as men who must give an account. Obey them so that their work will be a joy, not a burden, for that would be of no advantage to you" (Hebrews 13:17, NIV). Thank you, Lord, for direction and guidance. In Jesus' Name, Amen.

Question: *My Christian wife became very angry with a policeman she felt was treating her unjustly. She was so mad she threw something at him, accusing him of racial bigotry (she is from another country). This is not the first time she has been violently angry and fought with the police. When she came home, she was very upset, sobbing and repenting of her behavior. Now she has been issued a summons to appear in court. Can I bind the people in this situation to favoring her? She is not an American citizen and could be deported if she appears in court. I know God does not want our family torn apart. I think she is really sorry this time.*

Liberty's Answer: God knows exactly why this happened and what He wants to accomplish out of it. These prayer principles are not a means of getting God to do what we feel will be best, rather they are to get us into a position where God can work His will out in everyone involved. You should first pray the binding and loosing prayers exactly as they are written to hold yourself steady. Then you should bind your wife to God's will and loose wrong kinds of thinking that influenced what she did. She obviously has some serious problems with authority figures, perhaps policemen specifically.

You say she has become violent with policemen before without any serious consequences. God may have chosen this time to enroll her in His School of Consequences. Bind everyone involved—yourself, your wife, the policeman, the court officials, the judge, etc.—to God's will. Bind everyone's minds to the mind of Christ. You are asking my advice, and it is this: Don't try to use these prayers to influence what you think should happen! Loose any assignments of the enemy from everyone involved in this situation. Loose the stronghold thinking in your wife's soul that would try to justify her reaction to this policeman. Remember what God says in His Word about this:

> **"Remind the people to be subject to rulers and authorities, to be obedient, to be ready to do whatever is good, to slander no one, to be peaceable and considerate, and to show true humility toward all men"**
>
> (Titus 3:1-2, *NIV*).

Question: *What do you mean by soulish prayers? Isn't all prayer good, just as long as you are praying?*

Liberty's Answer: No, all prayers are not good! Pure prayer is, "Not my will regarding any part of this, God, but your will alone be done." Wrong agreements occur when you seek out others to pray soulish prayers with you:

1. to get support for a stand you are making,
2. to get others to take sides with your views, or
3. to support and help you make something happen.

God always moves with power in response to right agreements spoken, and the enemy always moves in response to wrong agreements spoken—especially those spoken in self-righteous, soulish prayers. Other examples of soulish prayers are people praying prayers to marry Judy or Betty or John or Jerry. I never agree with others on that kind of prayer. But I will pray with them and bind their wills, as well as Judy's and/or Jerry's wills (etc.), to the will of God. I will loose the effects and influences of all wrong prayers, all wrong agreements, and soul tie issues from everyone involved.

I have had many other people tell me something like, "We just love that young man over there, he's so sweet and so spiritual. We just know that he ought to be married to that young woman over there. So we get together every Thursday night and pray that they recognize that God wants the two of them to get married." God is the only one who knows the destiny purpose of that young man and that young woman. Do I think you can actually pray a self-targeted couple into a wrong marriage agreement? Not directly as a result of just prayer, but you certainly can begin to influence them to enter into wrong agreements with you if you are persuasive enough.

You can be praying for all kinds of things that look good to you but have nothing to do with God's plans and purposes. People who pray soulish prayers often put out information that they have spent a lot of time praying for things that happen. Rarely does anyone go around saying how much they have prayed for things that haven't happened, do they? We should always be ready to pray for others, always! But we should be less motivated to tell others how much we pray for them, unless they are asking us for such an assurance. We should be far more interested in praying anonymously.

I caution all of my intercessors to be very quiet about our prayers, unless someone needs reassurance that we are praying. God alone should get the glory for the answered prayers, not those who have prayed.

Question: *My family members treat me terrible. In fact, they treat most everyone terrible. I'm praying that they learn that they cannot do this and expect to be loved themselves. Will you agree on that with me?*

Liberty's Answer: No, I cannot. That would be what I call a soulish prayer seeking wrong agreement. Because the Lord loved you while you were still His enemy, you are obligated to love those others you feel are acting as enemies—especially if they are family members. No matter how badly they are acting towards you or others, this does not give you any justification for not praying for them in love. We must all grow in the Lord to the point where we refuse to allow the failings of others to change how we should feel and act towards them.

> *"There is no fear in love; but perfect love casts out fear, because fear involves torment. But he who fears has not been made perfect in love. We love Him because He first loved us. If someone says, 'I love God' and hates his brother, he is a liar; for he who does not love his brother whom he has seen, how can he love God whom he has not seen? And this commandment we have from Him: that he who loves God must love his brother also"*

(I John 4:18-21, *NKJV*).

Question: *I recently enjoyed attending one of your conferences. Twice now, I have heard you advise against praying for God to judge or punish our enemies. These are referred to as imprecatory prayers. Why then does David have so very many prayers of this type? How do you justify this apparent conflict with your opinion?*

59

Liberty's Answer: David did not have the Holy Spirit within him or the blood of Jesus shed for him. David did several things in the Old Testament that you not find any disciple or believer doing in the New Testament. He was a man of God and God's friend, but he was definitely a flawed "member" of God's family. He had a man assassinated so he could have his wife. He committed adultery. He impersonated a mad man to try to protect himself in Gath, even though the mentally ill of the day were thought to be demonically possessed. He had sunk so far from trusting God to take care of him that he impersonated God's worst enemy to try to hide who he was from the authorities.

In the New Testament, you will not find believers praying any of the prayers you have asked about. In one instance the disciples were highly upset that a village would not receive Jesus. James and John were so incensed that they said:

> ***Lord, do You want us to command fire to come down from heaven and consume them, just as Elijah did?' But He turned and rebuked them, and said, 'You do not know what manner of spirit you are of. For the Son of Man***

did not come to destroy men's lives but
to save them'
(Luke 9:54-56, *NKJV*).

In another passage of Scripture, Jesus said:

I tell you, Do not resist an evil person.
If someone strikes you on the right
cheek, turn to him the other also. And
if someone wants to sue you and take
your tunic, let him have your cloak as
well. If someone forces you to go one
mile, go with him two miles. Give to
the one who asks you, and do not turn
away from the one who wants to
borrow from you. You have heard that
it was said, 'Love your neighbor and
hate your enemy.' But I tell you: Love
your enemies and pray for those who
persecute you, that you may be sons
of your Father in heaven
(Matthew 5:39-45, *NIV*).

There is no room here for imprecatory prayers.
Jesus clearly called us all to love and to pray for the
good of all.

Question: *Last year at our church, we had a study of your books. I'm wondering if it is all right to loose poverty and its effects from our family and bind us to the prosperity (financial and otherwise) of God? I am continuing to bind our minds and wills to God and His truth.*

Liberty's Answer: It probably will not hurt anything to loose poverty and its effects from your family, but it probably won't help anything either. Financial lack is the outcome of wrong patterns of thinking about what money represents, wrong attitudes about what money can get, and wrong beliefs about who controls the source of all money. Wrong agreements spoken out of a family's poverty mentality can cause financial lack.

Negative spiritual influences always show up to take advantage of the access that wrong agreements create. Evil spirits have the right to inflict loss and pain upon individuals when a family is steeped in any kind of wrong agreements. Right agreements with God's principles cause the power of God to flow into a situation. Wrong agreements cause the power of darkness to flow into a situation.

Money is not the problem here. God can manifest money in any amount, anywhere, any time He wants to.

But what if an abundance of money would enable us to pursue our own desires which were only half a degree off from God's desires for us? Every step we took, our paths would angle further away from God's chosen path. So, our Father withholds money from His people until He knows they can see it as nothing more than a tool to use to accomplish His will. I read once where a man said that a wise man told him that everything he owned was either an idol or a tool to use for God. That's wisdom. I hope the following gives you some understanding of how best to pray.

> *Lord I bind myself and my family members, corporately or individually (as you lead me to pray), to your truth about money. I bind my mind and my family members' minds to the mind of Christ. Help all of us to know the truth of God's limitless resources and His Sovereign right to deal with each of His children in the ways He knows to be best.*

God does not have favorite people that He wants to bless with more money than others, but God does give money or allows money to be withheld to accomplish different purposes. Remember that the Bible does not say that money is the root of all evil, it says that the **love of money** is the root of all evil. The word *love*, as used here, encompasses wrong desires for what money can seem to provide, exceeding our desires for the things of the kingdom of God.

Question: *My daughter met a young man she felt was the one God wanted her to marry. One of my friends and I prayed about this, and after having visions about my daughter and this young man marrying, we felt this was God's will. My daughter and I prayed together about it with much fervency, especially after a prophetic word from a minister that seemed to confirm what we were praying about. We also heard preaching that said even if what you are believing to get from God looks impossible in the natural, don't give up.*

The young man has now walked away from God and has made many wrong choices, including marrying another woman. My daughter and I are devastated. I am certain this man knew that my daughter was chosen of God for him, but he rebelled. If we prayed wrong, then why did we have the visions, why were they confirmed by a minister who didn't know us, and why do we still feel this man is the one?

Liberty's Answer: I hope you have written to ask me this with the expectation of truth in my reply. You have indeed made wrong agreements and prayed wrong prayers, and thereby helped your daughter to believe in something that appears to have had nothing to do with God. To be very direct, you prayed soulish prayers with your friend and you prayed soulish prayers with your daughter. Such soulish praying almost always opens up doorways for deception, confusion, and soul ties. Soul ties are formed when agreements that have nothing to do with God's will are reached between human souls. The best thing to have prayed would have been to bind your daughter to the will and purposes of God for her life.

Your next step is to repent for trying (through your soulish prayers and your stand on what you thought was best) to get God to do what you and your daughter wanted. Then ask God to forgive you both. He will. It would also be a good thing to discuss this with your daughter and ask her to do the same thing and ask her to forgive you, as well. Then both of you should forgive this young man for his choices and actions. Then pray and bind him to God's will and release him. Let God work out His plans for his life.

> ***Wrong agreements were made, and wrong signs and confirmations seemed to come because people were praying soulish prayers. You were not praying that God's will would be done in each life.***

I can see your heart's love for your daughter, but your heart (soul) wants what <u>you</u> think would be best for her. The heart or soul, when left to its own devices rarely wants what God wants and knows is best for all the people involved in any situation. You have a chance here to see a real work of God as He cleans up the attempts of the enemy to capitalize on soulish prayers. Your "job" is to see that the effect and influences of those wrong agreements are broken, which you do by prayers of loosing them. Pray this:

> ***I loose all of the effects and influences of the wrong agreements that I have made, and any resulting soul ties that have been formed from them. Forgive me for having made them, Lord. Help me to pray purely for your will to be done on earth. Amen.***

My ministry and my books are focused on helping people see the difference between their born-again spirits and their unsurrendered souls. During our intercessors meeting, we prayed for you and your daughter. God is ready to put everything back on track with His will—not your will, and not your daughter's will—but His glorious and divine will! Please see if your daughter will pray the following general prayer, changing the pronouns to fit her desire for a mate. You can revise it, changing the pronouns to your daughter's name and pray it for her.

Jesus, if there is a special man/woman you have chosen and are preparing just for me, I bind him/her to your will and purposes. I ask that you draw him/her into a strong, whole relationship with you, Jesus. I ask that you teach him/her to see you as the focus and very center of his/her life, just as I am asking you to do with me. I bind myself and him/her to your timing. I will not seek to find any such person through my own efforts. You will know if and when the time is right for both of us to come together into a relationship.

Teach me how to love you, to bless you, and to minister to you. Teach me how to come apart from the world and go with you into that never-yet-entered secret meeting place that is just ours. Teach me how to receive whatever you want to give to me. In Jesus' name, Amen.

4

FINAL THOUGHTS

I asked God to give me happiness.
He said, No, that He had given blessings.
It was up to me to be happy about them.

I asked God to take away my pride.
He said, No, it was not for Him to take.
It was for me to surrender.

I asked God to grant me patience.

He said, No, patience is not granted.

It is gained by enduring tribulation.

Lord, please help us learn how to surrender our souls to you, that we would be ready to face the future. Help us to move onto our destiny tracks, that we would go forth with confidence in our steps. Teach us, Holy Spirit, how to pray right prayers, that we might impact our world. Amen.

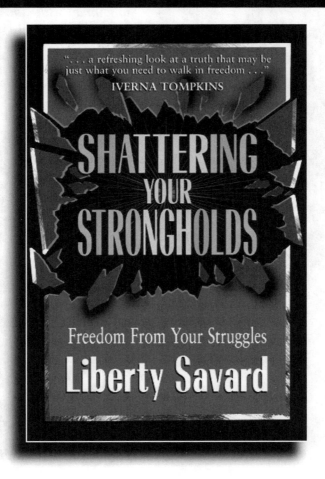

". . . a refreshing look at a truth that may be just what you need to walk in freedom . . ."

IVERNA TOMPKINS

SHATTERING YOUR STRONGHOLDS

Freedom From Your Struggles

Liberty Savard

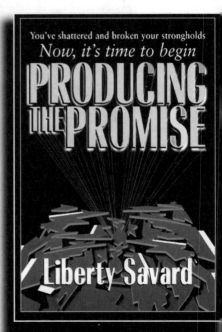